I0821255

Houston ASTROS

KENNY ABDO

Fly!
An Imprint of Abdo Zoom
abdobooks.com

abdobooks.com

Published by Abdo Zoom, a division of ABDO, P.O. Box 398166, Minneapolis, Minnesota 55439.

Printed in the United States of America, North Mankato, Minnesota.
102025
012026

Photo Credits: AP Images, Getty Images, Shutterstock
Production Contributors: Kenny Abdo, Jennie Forsberg, Grace Hansen
Design Contributors: Candice Keimig, Neil Klinepier

Library of Congress Control Number: 2025936780

Publisher's Cataloging-in-Publication Data

Names: Abdo, Kenny, author.
Title: Houston Astros / by Kenny Abdo
Description: Minneapolis, Minnesota : Abdo Zoom, 2026 | Series: MLB teams | Includes online resources and index.
Identifiers: ISBN 9798384940197 (lib. bdg.) | ISBN 9798384940951 (ebook) | ISBN 9798384941330 (read-to-me ebook)
Subjects: LCSH: Houston Astros (Baseball team)--Juvenile literature. | Baseball teams--Juvenile literature. | Professional sports--Juvenile literature. | Sports franchises--Juvenile literature. | Major League Baseball (Organization)--Juvenile literature.
Classification: DDC 796.357--dc23

Table of CONTENTS

ASTROS

The Houston Astros have blazed a trail through baseball history with its spectacular playing and roster of all stars in the Lone Star state!

STROS
71
HTX
71

ASTROS
WOOHOO!
Chevy
WALKER
8
HOUSTON ASTROS

With out-of-this-world skills and World Series titles, the Astros turn every game into a stellar showdown deep in the heart of Texas!

BATTER UP!

The Houston Astros began in 1962 as the Colt .45s. The team joined the **National League** (**NL**) and quickly became a part of Major League Baseball (MLB).

In 1965, the Colt .45s became the Astros. The new name honored Houston's link to space travel. The team's fresh look matched a city known for bold ideas and big dreams.

The Astros began to make big strides on the field. Jimmy Wynn hit more than 200 home runs and J. R. Richard led the league with 313 strikeouts in 1979.

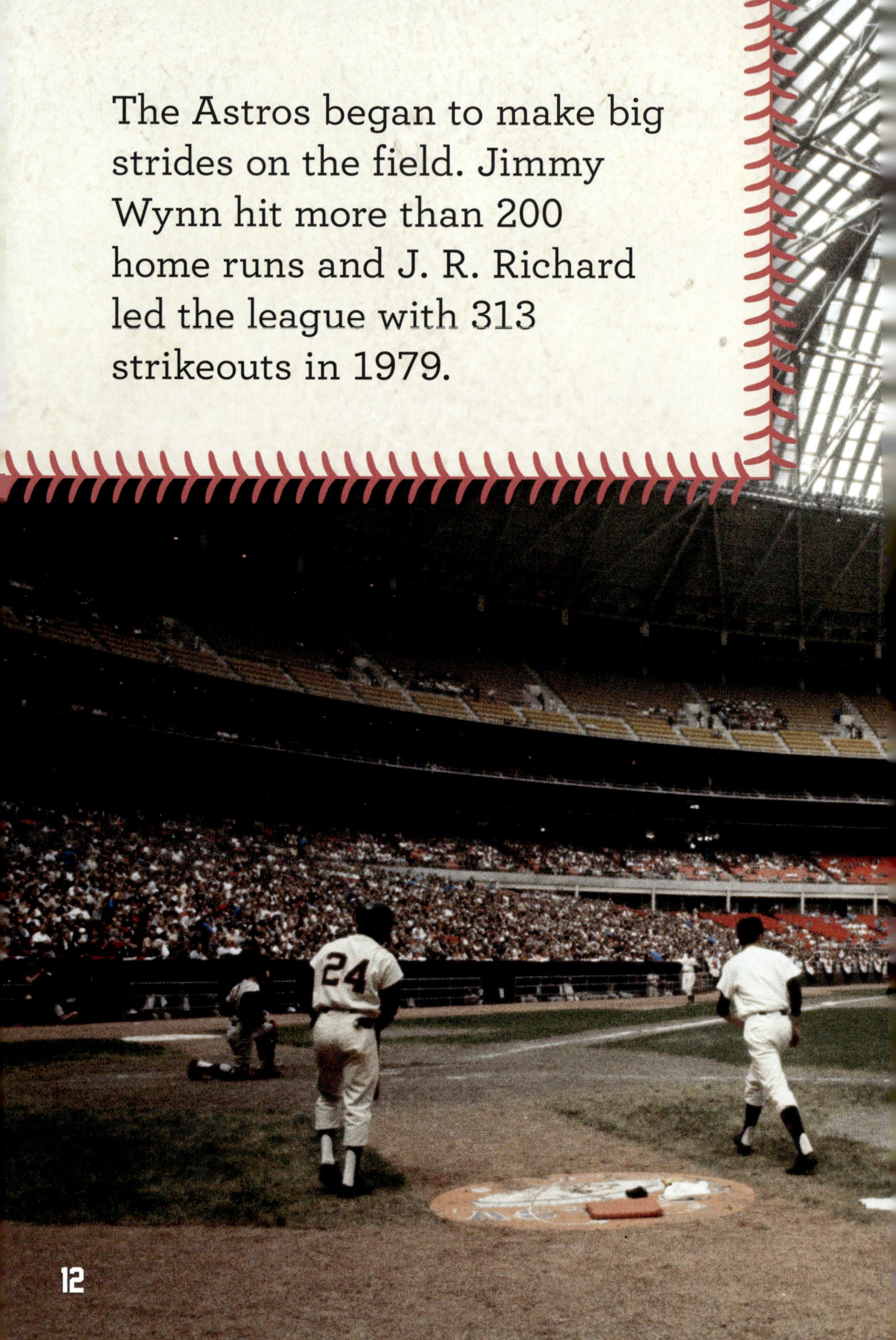

2:11
Gulf

GRAND SLAMS

The Astros reached its first postseason in 1980. However, the team would lose to the Phillies in the **NL** Championship Series. In 1997, the Astros won its first NL Central **Division** title.

The Astros reached the World Series for the first time in 2005 but lost to the White Sox in four games. In 2013, the team moved to the **American League** (**AL**). In 2017, the Astros' luck changed when they beat the Los Angeles Dodgers to win their first title!

Phillies
ASTROS
4

In 2019, the Astros returned to the World Series and showed off their talent, but lost to the Nationals in a close seven-game battle. In 2020, the Astros made headlines again, reaching the playoffs with a 29–31 **record**.

WORLD SERIES
CHAMPIONS
2022

The Astros launched a comeback after losing the 2021 World Series to the Braves. In 2022, they showed why they were one of the best teams in baseball. With strong pitching and smart play, the Astros won the **AL**, AL West, and the World Series!

The Astros celebrated their fourth straight **division** crown in 2024 after winning the **AL** West Championship. The Astros missed the 2025 playoffs for the first time since 2016. Fans hope Houston will be back on top.

ASTROS
2
OXY

HALL OF FAME

Craig Biggio spent his whole 20-year career with the Astros. He played both catcher and second base, showing his range of talent. Biggio had over 3,000 hits, made it to seven **All-Star** Games, and won four **Gold Gloves**. He entered the Baseball Hall of Fame in 2015.

AGWELL

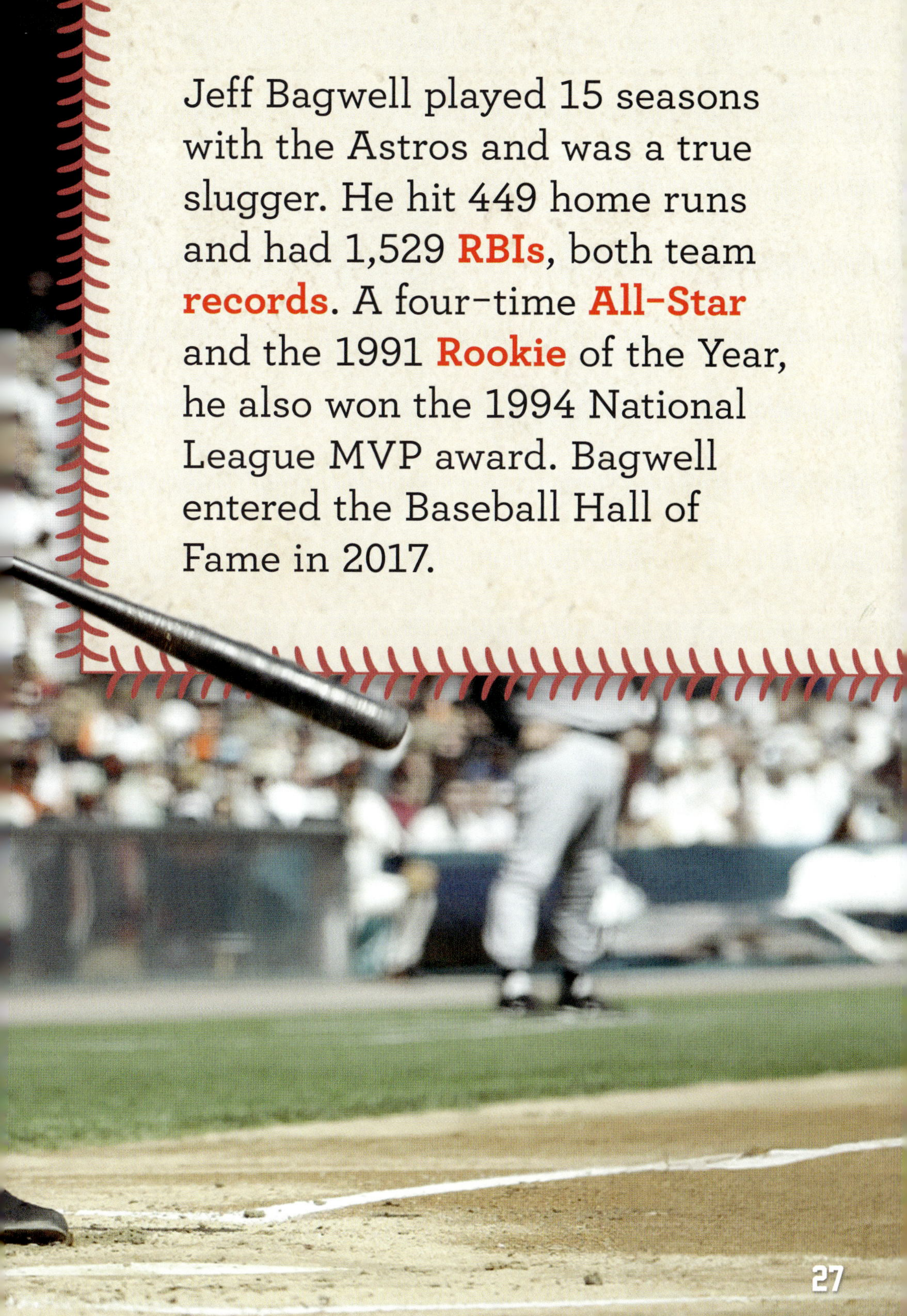

Jeff Bagwell played 15 seasons with the Astros and was a true slugger. He hit 449 home runs and had 1,529 **RBIs**, both team **records**. A four-time **All-Star** and the 1991 **Rookie** of the Year, he also won the 1994 National League MVP award. Bagwell entered the Baseball Hall of Fame in 2017.

José Altuve has played for the Astros since 2011 and has made a big impact with his strong skills. He is a nine-time **All-Star** and has won three batting titles. In 2017, he helped lead the Astros to their first World Series win! Altuve remains a key part of the team.

ASTROS
27

GLOSSARY

All-Star – a yearly baseball contest where top players from the AL and the NL compete against each other or an athlete named to the contest.

American League (AL) – one of two 15-team leagues that make up MLB.

division – a number of teams grouped together in a sport for competitive purposes.

Gold Glove Award – an annual award given to the best fielders at each position in both the AL and NL.

National League (NL) – one of two 15-team leagues that make up MLB.

record – a team's season total of wins and losses; a top achievement by a player or team that no one has done before.

Runs Batted In (RBI) – a statistic that credits a batter for making a play that allows a run to be scored.

rookie – a professional athlete in his or her first season in a sport.

ONLINE RESOURCES

To learn more about the Houston Astros, please visit **abdobooklinks.com** or scan this QR code. These links are routinely monitored and updated to provide the most current information available.

INDEX